I AM A BIG BRO

Hey there, Big Brother!
Let's play, laugh, and learn together!

Chloe Felix, a beloved author, brings joy to children with her engaging books. Her work inspires and ignites children's boundless imaginations and promotes skills development through delightful and educational content, nurturing a love for learning, creativity, and positive values.

Disclaimer:
This book is intended for entertainment purposes only. The activities, stories, and advice provided within are meant to be educational and fun, but should not be considered professional medical, psychological, or parenting guidance. The authors and publisher disclaim any liability arising directly or indirectly from the use of this book.

A LITTLE MESSAGE

Hi there, Big Brother!

My name is Chloe, and I'm so excited to be your guide on this fun journey of becoming an amazing big brother.

You're going to get a new best friend – a little brother or sister. Being an awesome big sibling is one of the most important jobs you'll ever have.

This book is filled with games, activities, stories, and ideas to help you prepare for your new brother or sister's arrival. It will teach you how to be a great helper, take care of your sibling, and have tons of fun together.

Being a big brother can be hard work sometimes, but also incredibly rewarding. Get ready for hugs, giggles, and a lifetime of adventures with your new partner!

Lots of love,

Chloe Felix

I am a
BIG BROTHER

My name is

....

I AM A
BIG BROTHER
NOW!

MY LITTLE SIBLING

Hello there, little one!
Your family has a brand new buddy.

This tiny friend is going to love all the kindness
and affection you have to share.

Let's give your newest playmate the
warmest welcome, filled with big hugs and smiles!

My little sibling

Baby's Name: ....
Birth Date: ....
Weight: ....
Height: ....
Gender: ☐ BOY ☐ GIRL

Heartwarming Notes: ....
....
....

THIS IS MY LITTLE SIBLING!

WINDY DAY FUN

Trace the lines to help the kites fly in the sky!

LINE ADVENTURE

Trace along the lines to help the big brother reach the baby!

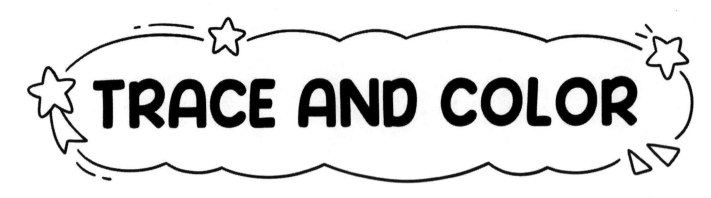

TRACE AND COLOR

Trace the drawing to complete the picture!

SNAIL SHELLS

The snails need your help to make their little homes.
Trace the lines to complete their shells.

Protect your sibling
like a shell protects the tiny snail inside.

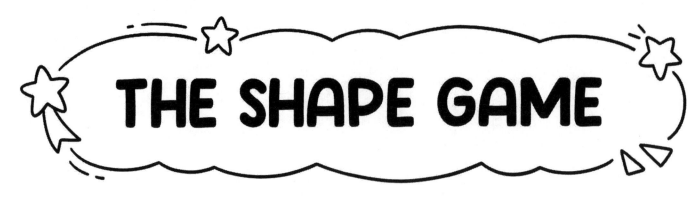

THE SHAPE GAME

Look at the shape at the top of each row
and find the thing that matches it.

Offer a favorite toy or stuffed animal to comfort
and distract your little sibling when upset.

COLOR THE SHAPES

Each shape has a secret color clue next to it.
Find and color the shapes with the matching colors.

◯ = Yellow   ☐ = Red   △ = Green   ▭ = Blue

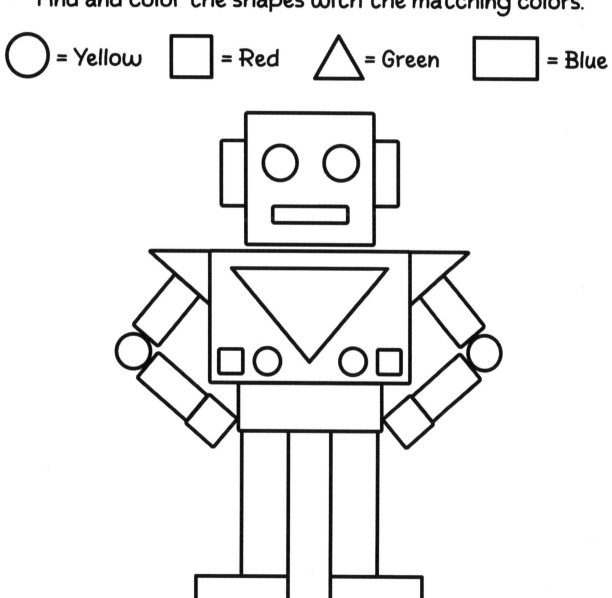

Being a big brother is like being a cool robot,
always ready to help and protect your little sibling.

BIG BROTHER CAPE

Let's color the cape and celebrate your special role!

BIG BROTHER

The Big Brother cape is where you get your
special powers to be the best big kid ever.
Your cape gives you the power
to make your sibling feel safe and loved.

SIBLING SEARCH

Draw a line to connect each big brother animal with their little sibling.

   •   •

   •   •

   •   •

    •   •

   •   •

   •   •

NAME CRACKERS

Find the snacks with the letters in your name
and your sibling's name.

GET HOME TOGETHER!

Help the big brother and his little sibling
to find the way out to their mommy.

WHAT COMES NEXT?

Look at the patterns carefully.
What do you think comes next?

AWESOME BIG BROTHER

Being a big brother is an important job, and I love it!

Sometimes, Mom and Dad have to spend a lot of time taking care of my little sibling

BUT!!

BIG BROTHER

THERE ARE SO MANY THINGS I CAN DO TO HELP!

AWESOME BIG BROTHER

LEARN BABY SIGNS

Baby signs are fun little hand moves that help babies share what they want before they can talk.

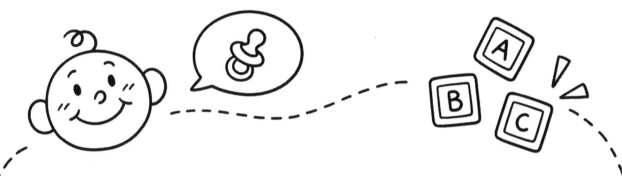

- **Pick a fun sign!** Start with something the baby often uses, like "milk" or "eat."

- **Make the sign BIG and SLOW.** Show the baby your hand and say the word clearly at the same time. Like "Milk!" (fist with thumb out).

- **Do it again and again!** The more you play, the faster the baby will learn.

- **Be patient!** It might take a while for the baby to sign back. But keep playing, and they'll get it!

YES
Make a fist and move it up and down like you're nodding your head up and down to say "yes".

NO
Stick out your thumb, index finger, and middle finger. Snap them together quickly.

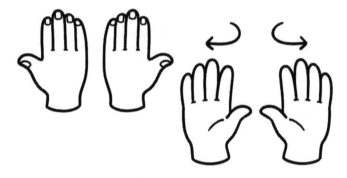

ALL DONE
Start with your palms facing you, then turn your hands so your palms face out.

MILK
Make a fist with one hand, open it a little, then make a fist again. Repeat.

EAT
Tap your fingers to your mouth.

SLEEP

Start with your hand open in front of your face. Slowly move your hand down to your chin and close your fingers. Make a sleepy face while doing it.

WATER

Hold up three fingers in the middle, with your thumb and pinkie down. Tap your index finger on your chin a couple of times.

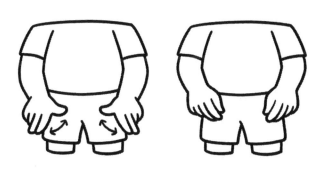

DIAPER

Make a pinching motion with your hand, like you're grabbing a diaper.

MOMMY

Tap your thumb on your chin.

DADDY

Tap your thumb on your forehead.

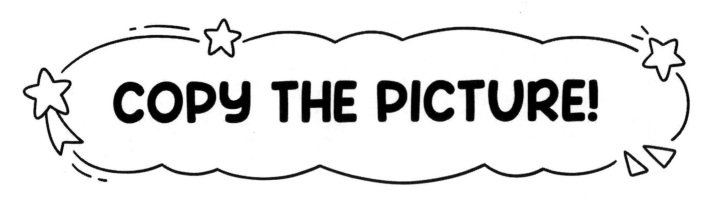

COPY THE PICTURE!

Look at the picture on the grid
and try to draw it just like you see it!

A big brother's love is like a shield,
keeping his sibling safe and sound.

MISSING HALF

Draw the other part of each picture to finish it!

Every picture needs both halves,
just like your brother or sister needs you.

BROTHERSAURUS

LIKE A NORMAL BROTHER BUT MORE ROARSOME

Connect the nine dots to copy the pattern.

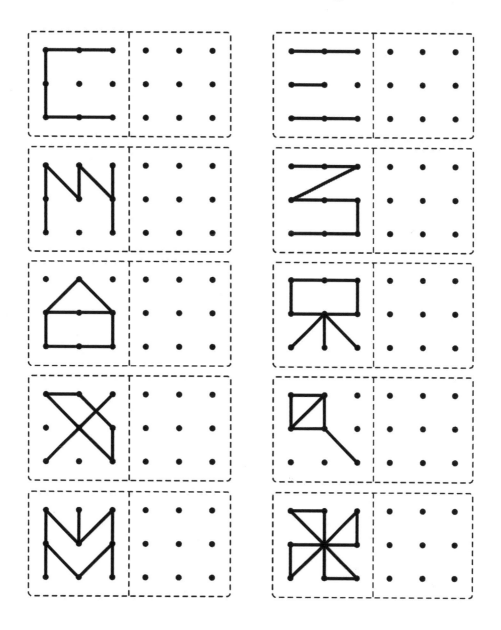

You can play with your little sibling
and build a special bond full of love and fun.

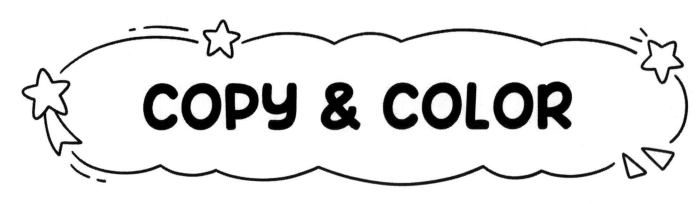

COPY & COLOR

Copy the pretty picture onto the next page,
then use your crayons to make it colorful!

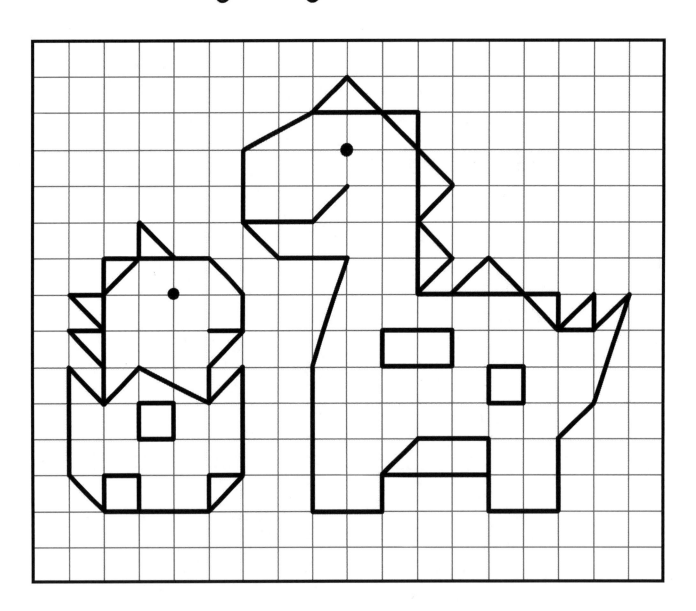

Protect your little dinosaur,
just like a big dino looks after the smaller ones.

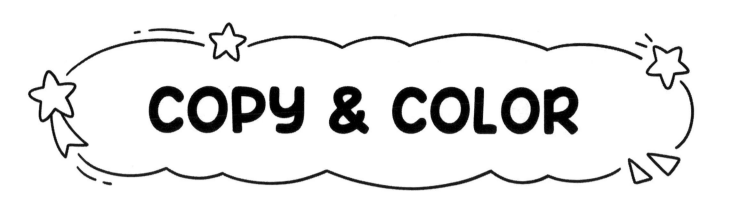

COPY & COLOR

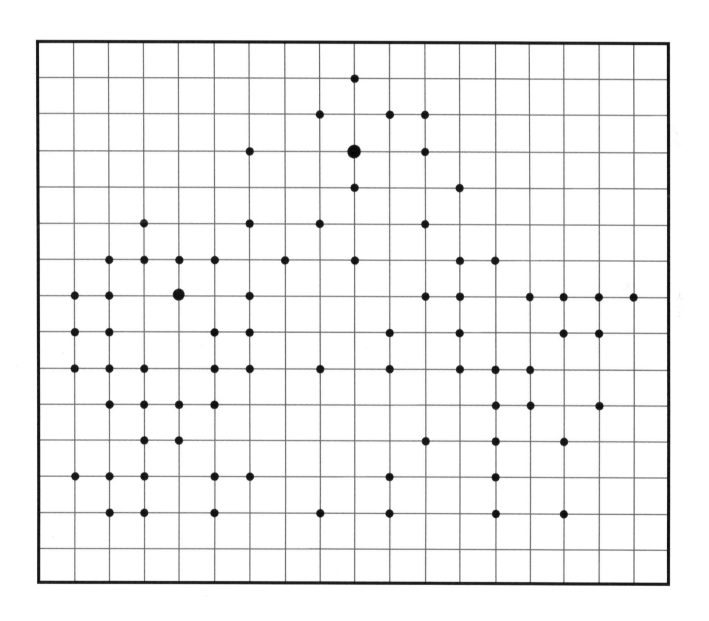

PAIR THE OPPOSITES

Draw a line to connect each word with its opposite.

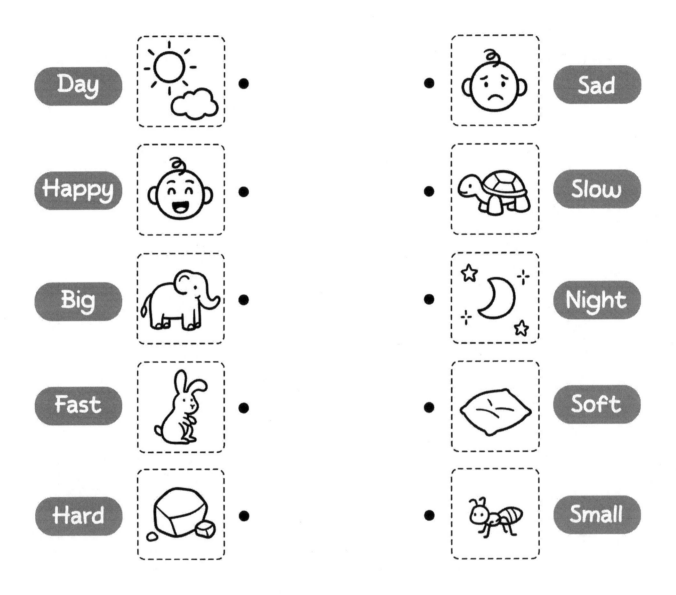

Day

Happy

Big

Fast

Hard

Sad

Slow

Night

Soft

Small

Big brothers and young siblings are like sunshine
and rain. Sometimes the rain clouds bring tears,
but together they create the most beautiful rainbows.

FOLLOW THE PATH!

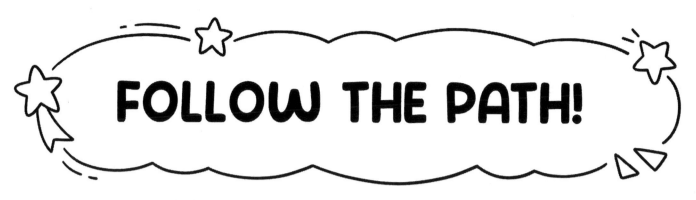

Who can get to the baby sibling?
Follow the trails and find out who wins the race!

FOLLOW THE HEARTS

Follow the pretty heart path through the awesome maze to find the baby sibling.

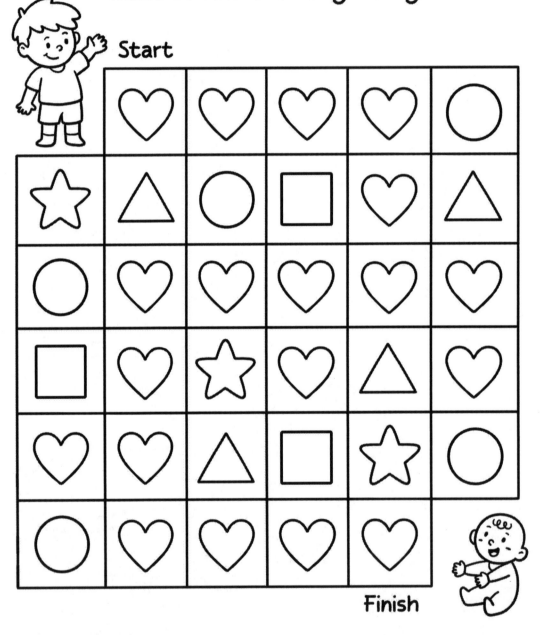

Being a big brother means showing love daily, like giving big hugs and sharing smiles.

BEYOND THE MESS: A BROTHER'S LOVE

BEYOND THE MESS: A BROTHER'S LOVE

BEYOND THE MESS: A BROTHER'S LOVE

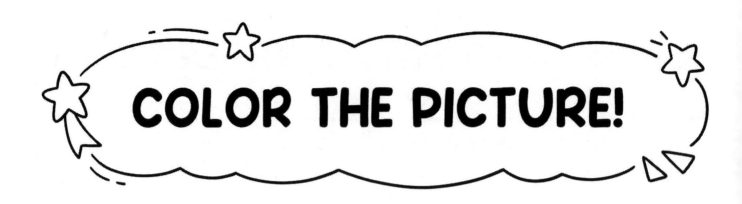

COLOR THE PICTURE!

Bond with your sibling by playing and having fun together, just like good friends who care about each other.

FIND THE TREASURE!

Guide the big brother and his little sibling to find the treasure by going through all the mazes!

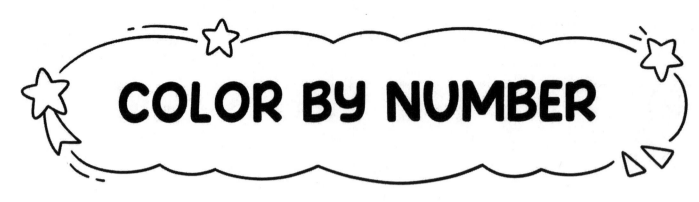

COLOR BY NUMBER

Color the picture following the numbers!

1 – Yellow   2 – Orange   3 – Pink

4 – Green   5 – Blue

Protect your little sibling from danger,
like a big lion keeps its family safe.

HAPPY AFFIRMATIONS!

Affirmations are nice things we can say to ourselves. They remind us how awesome and one-of-a-kind we are.
When we say them, it's like giving ourselves a big, cozy hug with our words!

I'm a great helper.

I'm so proud to be big!

I'm patient and gentle.

I am a good role model.

I am helpful to my parents.

I am strong and brave.

I am caring and supportive.

I have a big, loving heart.

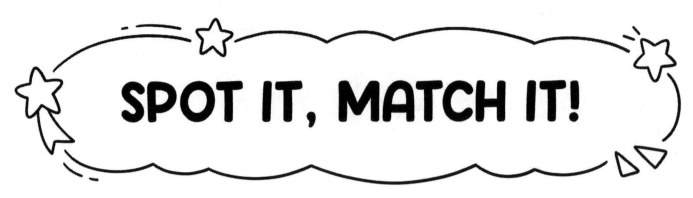

SPOT IT, MATCH IT!

Find the animal that matches each print
and pair them up.

40

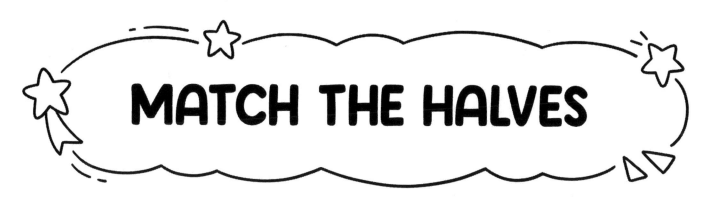

MATCH THE HALVES

Match the halves to complete the animal pictures!

Be patient and kind, just like matching
puzzle pieces gently and carefully.

WHAT IS IT?

Look at the clue, guess what it is,
and circle the correct answer!

Being a big brother is like being a super detective!
You use your super senses to guess what your little
buddy needs to feel happy.

CONNECTED BY HEARTS

Connect the dots from 1 to 10 to complete the picture.

HAPPY MEMORIES

Color the picture using your favorite colors.

You can have lots of fun with your little brother or sister!
Playing together will make you both so happy and laugh!

BIG BROTHER SAVES THE DAY

Mommy and Daddy look sleepy from taking care of the baby all day.

Maybe I can help so they can rest!

BIG BROTHER SAVES THE DAY

BIG BROTHER SAVES THE DAY

BIG BROTHER'S GUIDE

You can be the best big brother!
Help mommy and daddy with the baby.
Do little things like hold the bottle or get diapers.
Mommy and Daddy will be so happy! You are very helpful.

Read baby sweet stories

Sing pretty songs for bedtime

Give baby yummy food and play fun games

Help change dirty diapers and splash in the tub

Snuggle and cuddle the baby when they cry

Pick up baby's toys

Give baby lots of hugs and kisses!

THE BABY IS SLEEPING!

Find the 7 differences between the two pictures.
Circle each difference you spot.

Try not to make loud noises or sudden movements
near the baby's sleeping area.

FIND THE LOST PIECES

Some parts are gone. Find the right parts to make
the picture whole and write their numbers in the empty spots.

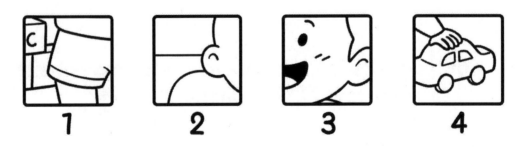

SOOTHING RHYMES

Read a poem that rhymes softly to help
the baby relax and sleep peacefully.

Twinkle, twinkle, little friend,
It's time for the day to end.
Close your eyes and drift away,
Dreams will come to you to play.

Twinkle, twinkle, night is here,
Stars are dancing, moon is near.
Rest your head and feel so light,
Sleep until the morning bright.

Twinkle, twinkle, sleep so tight,
Till the sun shines warm and bright.
Dream of laughter, dream of play,
Until you wake to a brand new day.

BATH TIME HELPER

Let's help Dad prepare for the baby's bath!
Find the baby soap, onesie, towel, and rubber ducky.

MATCHING SHADOWS

Find and circle the correct shadow of each food.

Share snacks and meals with your sibling,
matching their favorite foods to make them happy.

HELP MOM MAKE DINNER!

Look at each number and circle the group
with the same number of things.

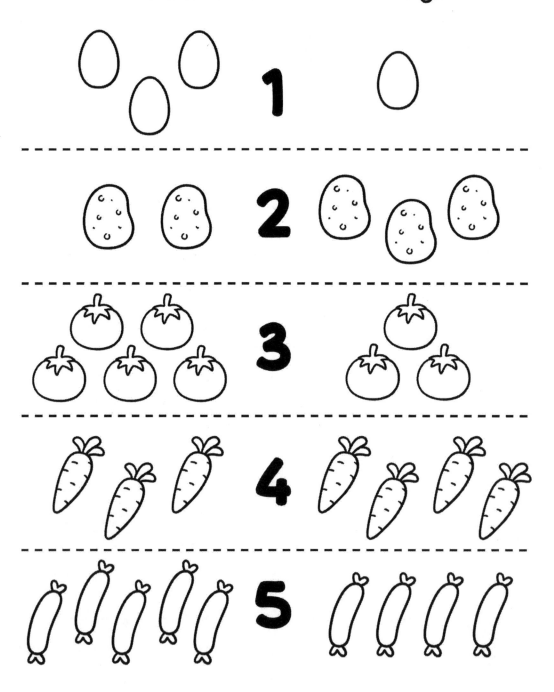

NARROW OR WIDE

Circle the right narrow or wide pictures
based on the questions!

Which door is wide?

Which book is narrow?

Which sofa is wide?

Which window is wide?

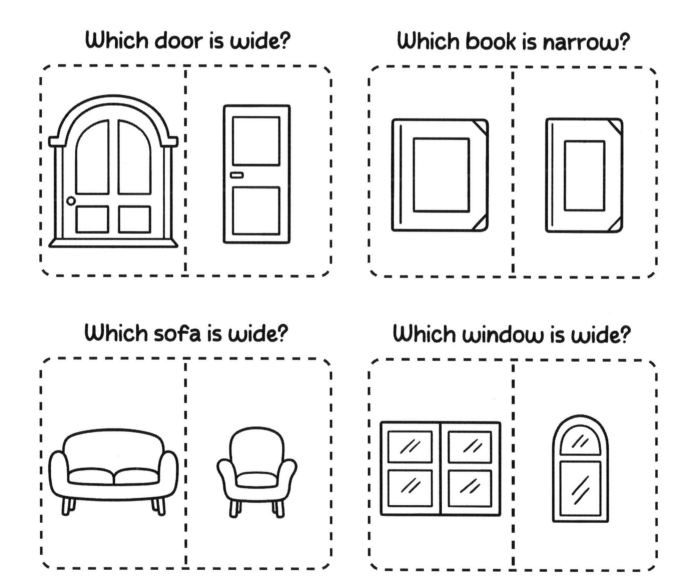

FINDING HOME

Help these siblings find their home?
Draw a line to show where they live!

THE "BIGGEST ONE"

Look at each group of things
and circle the biggest one.

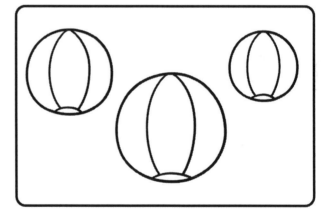

MAKE MOM SMILE

Mommy is tired from taking care of the baby.
Let's take her some yummy treats to make her happy!
Color the snacks to make Mom happy!

FIND THE TOYS

Your little sibling had so much fun playing,
but the toys are all over the place!
Let's help Mommy find all the lost toys!

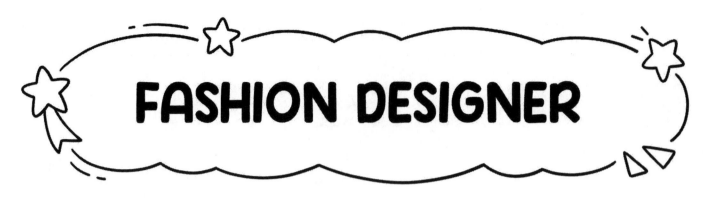

FASHION DESIGNER

These clothes lost their pretty pictures after getting washed. Let's draw new designs to make them look cool!

SORT THE CLOTHES!

Time to help Mommy!
Let's find the thing that doesn't go with the others.

SOCK MATCH-UP MISSION

Mommy is taking care of the baby right now.
Let's help her by finding the socks that go together!

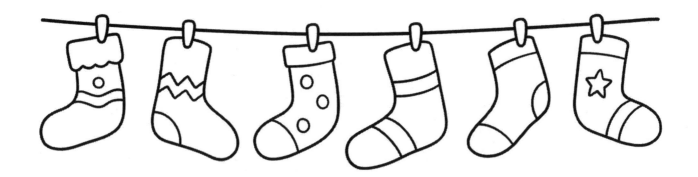

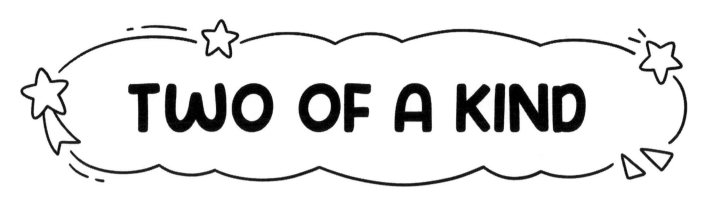

TWO OF A KIND

Look closely! One thing shows up two times.
Can you spot it?

DADDY'S LITTLE HELPER

Daddy needs to put a fresh, clean diaper on the baby! Let's find a new diaper for Daddy.

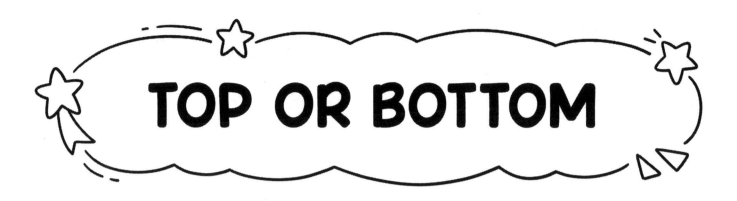

TOP OR BOTTOM

Circle the shark on the bottom.

Circle the guinea pig on the top.

Circle the dinosaur on the bottom.

Circle the dragon on the top.

FIND THE GROCERIES

Let's help Daddy find all the foods on his shopping list.
Use your sharp eyes to spot everything on his list!

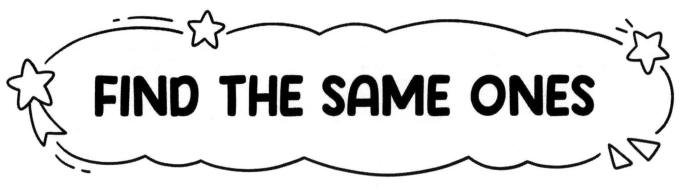

FIND THE SAME ONES

Mommy is home from shopping!
Let's help Mommy put everything away!
Can you find the items that look just like
the ones we already have?

HEAVIEST OBJECT

Look at each set of two pictures.
Find the heavier one and draw a circle around it!

THE BIGGEST GROUP

Each box has 2 groups of animals.
Let's count how many animals are in each group.
Then, circle the group with more animals.

TIDY UP TIME

Let's help Mommy clean up the room!
Follow the numbers from 1 to 9 to collect all the toys.

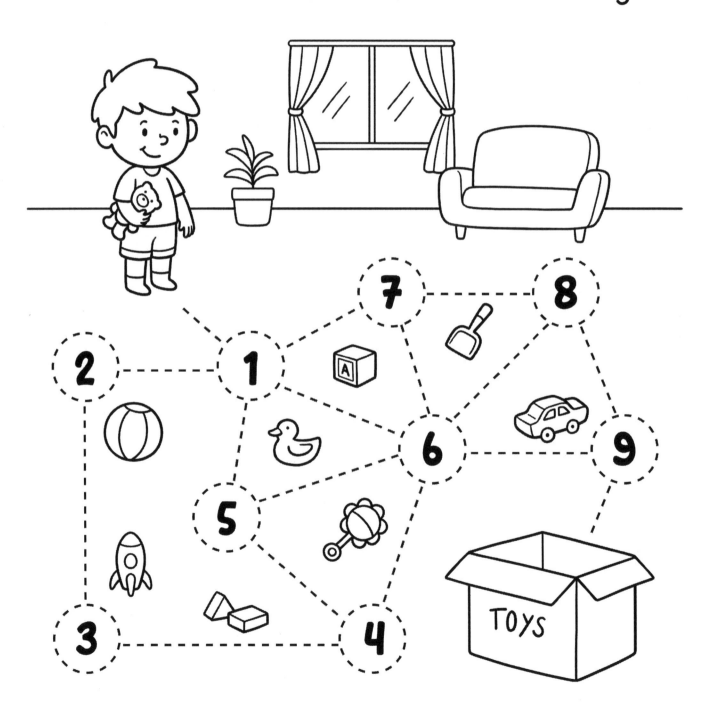

TOY SHADOW MATCH

Match the toys with their shadows.

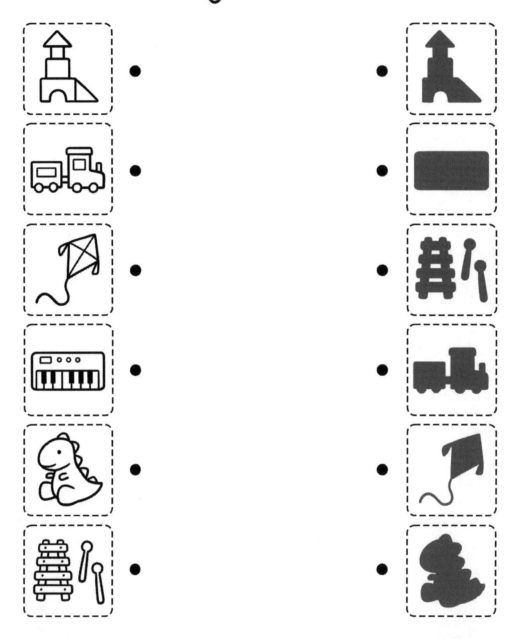

Share your toys with your sibling and enjoy
laughing together to create wonderful memories.

CIRCLE THE COZY CLOTHES

Help the big brother and his little
sibling prepare to play in the snow!
Circle all the winter clothes and accessories.

SUMMER SEEK AND COUNT

Can you spot all the summer items?
Count how many you see of each!

Think about all the happy playtimes you and your baby brother or sister can have this sunny season!

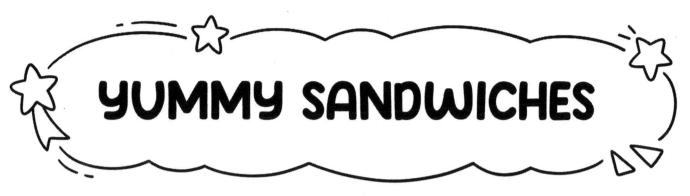

YUMMY SANDWICHES

Let's help Mom make sandwiches by drawing peanut butter and jelly on these bread slices.

When your mommy looks tired, you can help her in the kitchen. But only do things that are safe for you.

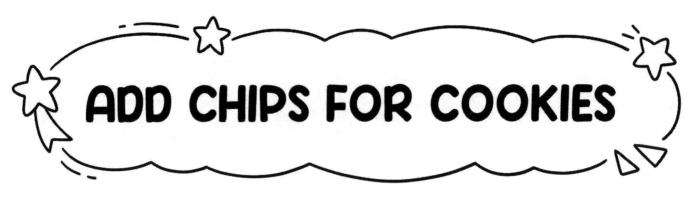

ADD CHIPS FOR COOKIES

Let's help Mom make yummy cookies.
Count the number next to each cookie
and add that many chocolate chips!

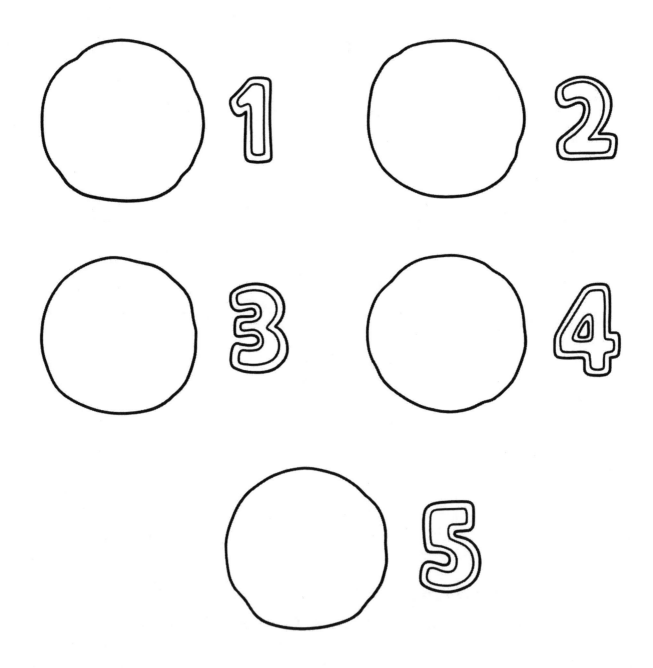

THE CARING BIG BROTHER

THE CARING BIG BROTHER

THE CARING BIG BROTHER

As days go by, with a little try and try, my sibling will get the hang of it, just like I once did.

And when I'm there to help, smiles pop up on our faces!

COLORING FUN!

Sometimes sharing isn't easy, but remember,
you get a special partner for playtime adventures!

FOOD PUZZLE

Can you find the pieces to make these
yummy foods whole?

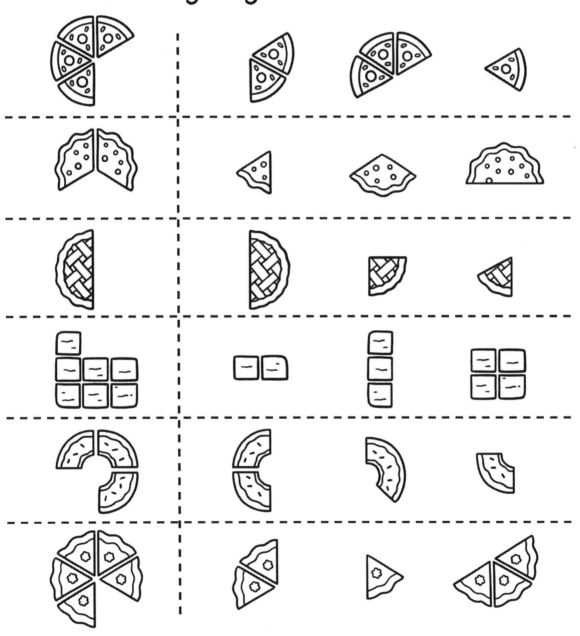

Use your big brother hugs to comfort and cheer up
your sibling, because you're their missing piece of joy.

BEDTIME MAZE

Let's lend Mommy a hand in putting your younger sibling to bed! Can you find the way to the cozy bed?

FAIRY TALE FUN

Look at each row of pictures from a fairy tale.
Find the one that does not belong.

Share your favorite storybooks with your sibling,
making storytime special and happy.

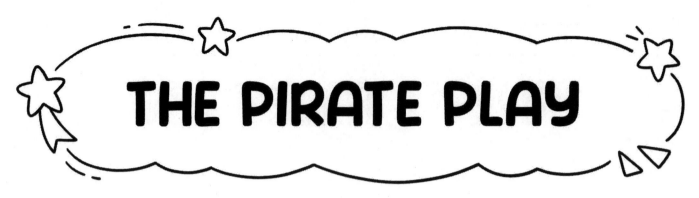

THE PIRATE PLAY

Let's color this picture like a masterpiece!

Play pretend together and imagine wild
adventures, because having a little sibling
is like having the best playmate.

SPOT THE SILLY!

Look closely at each picture.
Can you spot something funny or weird?

FIRST, NEXT, LAST!

Look at the pictures and think about the story they tell. Put 1 in the box for what happens first, 2 for what comes next, and 3 for the last part of the story.

MAZE CHALLENGE

Can you help the big brothers find their little one?

LONG OR SHORT

Circle the big brother with the short pants.

Circle the little sibling with the long bib.

Circle the dad with the short beard.

Circle the mom with the long dress.

Big brothers can be tall, and little siblings might be short, but their love for each other is endless.

FIND THE TALLEST!

Look at each group and find the tallest object.
Draw a circle around it.

Show your sibling how to grow tall and strong,
like a big brother who knows how to help.

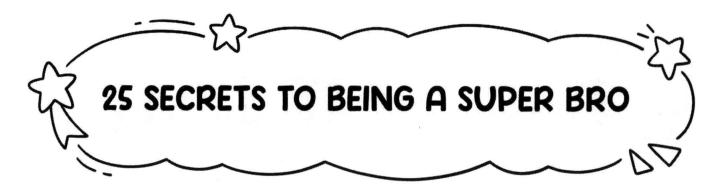

25 SECRETS TO BEING A SUPER BRO

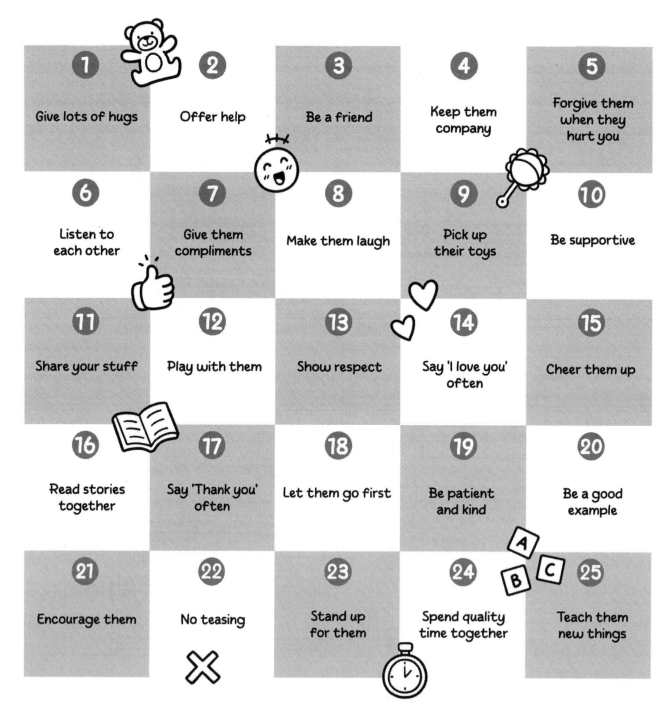

1 Give lots of hugs	**2** Offer help	**3** Be a friend	**4** Keep them company	**5** Forgive them when they hurt you
6 Listen to each other	**7** Give them compliments	**8** Make them laugh	**9** Pick up their toys	**10** Be supportive
11 Share your stuff	**12** Play with them	**13** Show respect	**14** Say 'I love you' often	**15** Cheer them up
16 Read stories together	**17** Say 'Thank you' often	**18** Let them go first	**19** Be patient and kind	**20** Be a good example
21 Encourage them	**22** No teasing	**23** Stand up for them	**24** Spend quality time together	**25** Teach them new things

Congratulations, little man!

You finished this activity book like a champ. All those games, puzzles, and activities have prepared you to be the ultimate Big Brother superhero.

Pretty soon, your little sibling is going to think you're the coolest big brother ever. Why? Because you're going to teach them all the best games, show them how to build epic forts, and keep them laughing with your amazing jokes.

Having a little brother or sister is like gaining a sidekick for life! You two will have so many adventures and make incredible memories together. Just remember, with great big brotherhood comes great responsibility – so keep being the awesome and caring guy you are.

High five, Big Bro!

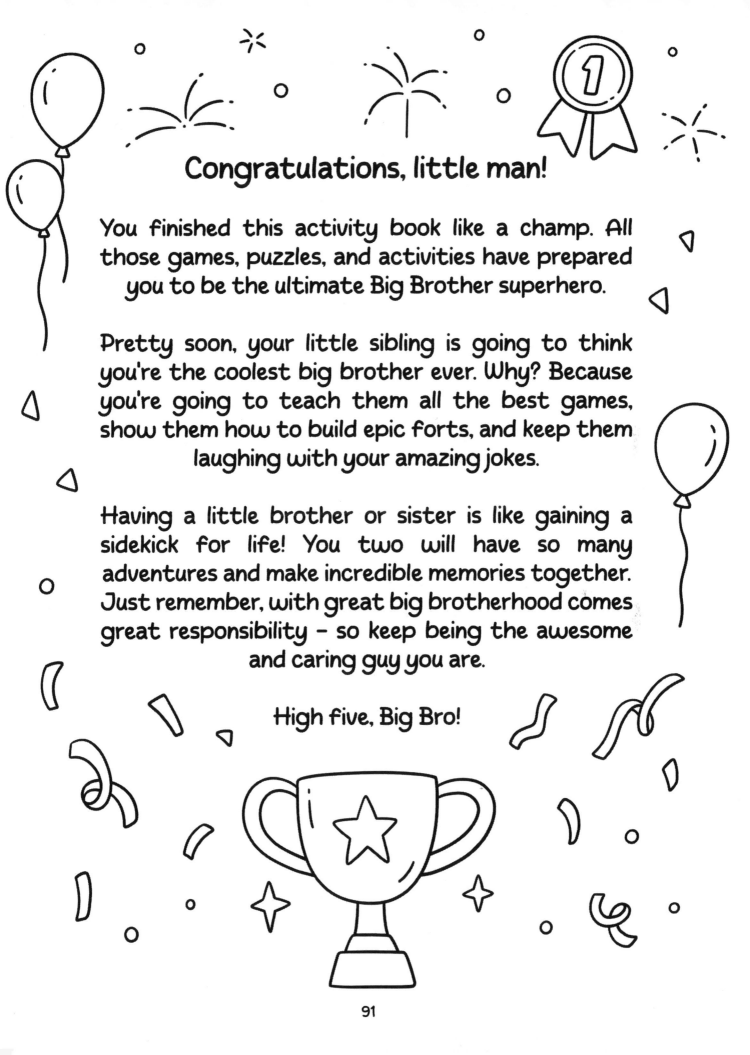

THE SHAPE GAME

SIBLING SEARCH

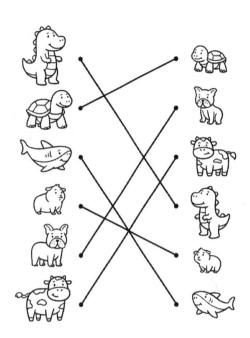

GET HOME TOGETHER!

WHAT COMES NEXT?

PAIR THE OPPOSITES

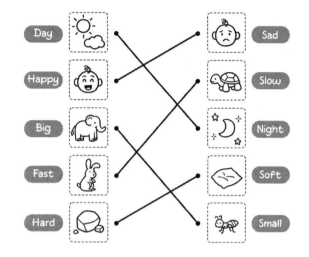

FOLLOW THE PATH!

FOLLOW THE HEARTS

FIND THE TREASURE!

SPOT IT, MATCH IT!

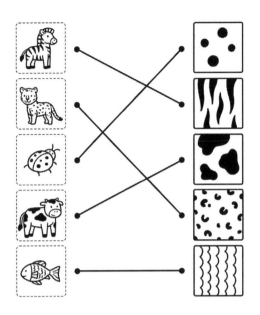

MATCH THE HALVES

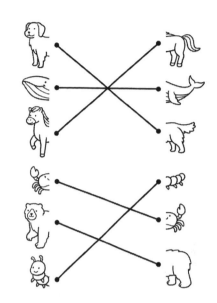

WHAT IS IT?

THE BABY IS SLEEPING!

FIND THE LOST PIECES

BATH TIME HELPER

MATCHING SHADOWS

HELP MOM MAKE DINNER!

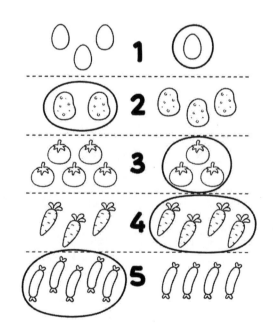

NARROW OR WIDE

Which door is wide?   Which book is narrow?

Which sofa is wide?   Which window is wide?

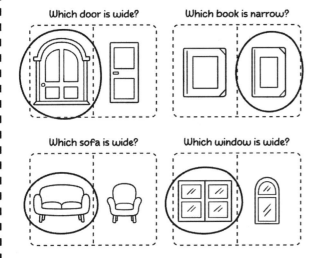

FINDING HOME

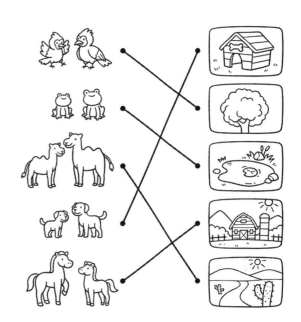

THE "BIGGEST ONE"

FIND THE TOYS

SORT THE CLOTHES!

SOCK MATCH-UP MISSION

TWO OF A KIND

DADDY'S LITTLE HELPER

TOP OR BOTTOM

Circle the shark on the bottom.

Circle the guinea pig on the top.

Circle the dinosaur on the bottom.

Circle the dragon on the top.

FIND THE GROCERIES

FIND THE SAME ONES

HEAVIEST OBJECT

THE BIGGEST GROUP

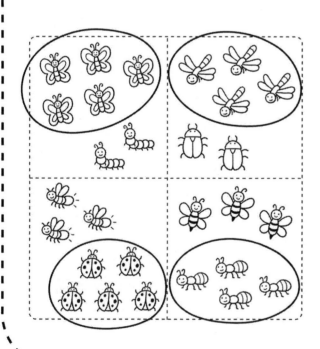

TIDY UP TIME

TOY SHADOW MATCH

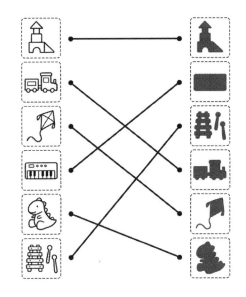

CIRCLE THE COZY CLOTHES

SUMMER SEEK AND COUNT

ADD CHIPS FOR COOKIES

 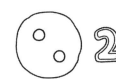

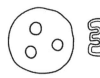

FOOD PUZZLE

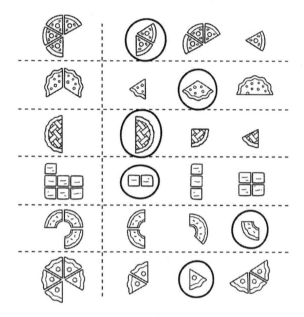

BEDTIME MAZE

FAIRY TALE FUN

SPOT THE SILLY!

FIRST, NEXT, LAST!

MAZE CHALLENGE

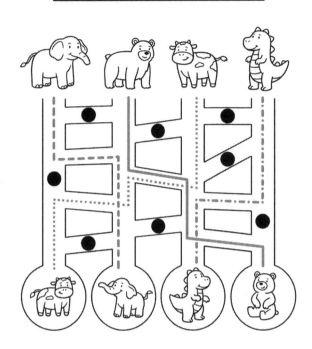

LONG OR SHORT

FIND THE TALLEST!

Made in the USA
Columbia, SC
13 December 2024

49202891R00057